Dreams for Breakfast

Dreams for Breakfast
Susan Millar DuMars

salmonpoetry

Published in 2010 by
Salmon Poetry
Cliffs of Moher, County Clare, Ireland
Website: www.salmonpoetry.com
Email: info@salmonpoetry.com

ISBN 978-1-907056-35-2

Cover artwork: *White One*, acrylic on canvas, by Anne O'Byrne
Cover design & typesetting: *Siobhán Hutson*
Printed in England by imprint*digital*.net

Published with financial assistance from the Arts Council

for my brother

Acknowledgements

Acknowledgements are due to the following publications, in which some of these poems previously appeared:

Crannóg, Ouroborous Review, Natural Bridge, Raintown Review, ROPES, Landing Places Anthology (Dedalus, 2010).

"I Dream of Sarah Palin" took second place in a slam at Chicago's Green Mill, February 2009.

No writer is an island. This book wouldn't exist without the support of my skilled friends and colleagues, including: John Walsh and Lisa Frank, Lorna Shaughnessy, Celeste Augé, Mary Madec, Susan Lindsay, all in the Writers' Keep, all in the Galway Arts Centre Thursday workshop, Karin Grieve, Ger Ward, Dimitris Lyacos, Patrick Chapman, Eamonn and Dru Wall. As always my love and gratitude to Jessie Lendennie, Siobhán Hutson, and Jean Kavanagh of Salmon; and to my husband, Kevin.

Contents

DREAMS

Belfast, April 1941	13
Dreams for Breakfast	15
I Dream of Sarah Palin	16
Winning	17
Vacant Building	19
Plans	20
Storm in Athens	22
The Past *(I & II)*	23
The Way You Die Again In My Dreams	25
Outside the Crane Bar *(I – V)*	26
Penitents	31
Going At It	32
Ten Years In	33
Granny	34
Missing Tom	35
Taillights	36
Connie	38
Beatrice	39
I Dream of Stephen Fry	41
I Dream My Mouth	42
Rooms	43

BREAKFAST

Coffee	47
Juliet's Roommate Speaks	48
WAY OUT	49
St. Louis, November 2008	50
I Learn To Write	51
Skates	52
But No Man Moved Me – till the Tide	53
Plato's Ghost	54
Make Me An Instrument	55
Ladybug	56
#30 Mexico Plum	57
Philadelphia, August 1966	58
Blessing	59
About the Author	61

Dreams

Belfast, April 1941

Susie Millar of Mackie Street,
the tall tales we tell of bombs
involve your husband Dusty with his pint
staring down the IRA. No one seems
to have taken down your story.

you emerge from the piss-smelling darkness
from the hole full of weeping
climb a ladder into light
eye pricking grey-white
you must have squinted
even cloudy light
is light

a child tugs on each hand
your belly swelling
you step aside to let others pass

smell of meat cooking
woman sobbing *Paul*
Paul

glimpse of staring eyes
a dust-caked face before
they cover it
with a blanket

merry crackle of flames
so much light

the world changed
all you knew
the light comes through
empty windows

walls with nothing behind them
salt on your lips
you didn't know you were crying
so much light

you walk
through the city
like so many others
looking for something familiar —

she emerges
from the dark pickling of your womb
her cave from which she'd eavesdropped
adds her thin mewl to the mix

the air raid sirens
the shattering glass
the booms

Dreams for Breakfast

Sometimes everything is blue;
the hills, my hands,
house keys, chimney smoke.
If I bit the air
my mouth would fill with blue juice.
I'm peaceful, though I wonder,
what casts such a big shadow?

Or I'm on a bus
with plaid seat covers.
The other passengers
are wilted, short
of breath. I think
I missed my stop.

Other times I walk through
a silent city of stone
and nothing is where I remember
except the swans
and the church on the hill.

I unwrap these dreams
for you over breakfast.
You say they are big budget,
Technicolour
while yours are pocket sized,
abridged; small men
in smaller circumstances.
You butter the toast and laugh.

I smile, marooned
in all this blue distance.

I Dream Of Sarah Palin

She tearfully tells Tom Brokaw
what bothers her is the effect media sniping
has had on her Amy.
I am, after all, a mother first.
Tom rises to his feet, shouting,
Amy was Jimmy Carter's daughter! Not yours!

Sarah, not one held back by details,
wink/shrugs *whatever.*
Tom unsheathes a samurai sword he keeps beneath
his desk – and as the crew encircles them, cheering,
You betcha!
he slices her head clean off

and drop-kicks it into Wasilla Lake.
The ratings go through the gosh-darn roof!
The head spins and bounces along the sea bed.
The Discovery Channel films clouds of fish
weaving in and out of the bubbles.

And all those little Americanisms,
the gee whiz thumbs up catalogue,
they lose their smirk; climb the cold waves
and SHOUT OUT from the clean surface of the water
(and their cry is heard from Russia's coast
to what used to be New Orleans),
United States, reclaim us! Take us back to your rec rooms
and your gold station wagons. We belong to you.
Don't let us be used against you.

Meanwhile, back on land,
Sarah's corpse sprouts a new head
and just keeps right on talking.

Winning

It slid from its red velvet pouch,
pulsed on my father's fleshy palm,
blazing gold.
My own face in each scored side.

My father demonstrated, rotated
sections; with humble clicks
the squares assumed their new positions.
The sound of tumblers
in a combination lock.
My father's hands
warmed the brass
as he worked.

When he finally let me hold it
it was nearly hot.

The others called it pointless,
a waste of time and money.
Words that stuck to my father
like warning labels.

What's the use, they asked,
of a Rubik's cube
that's all one colour?

I loved
its reassuring heat, its heft,
its sheen.
I understood
why Dad stayed
in his chair at the table
long after the rest
had moved to the TV

and turned and turned
and turned. And every time
the pieces found their places,
with each soft click he'd whisper
to himself,
I win!

Vacant Building

All we had wanted was something better.
Marble countertops, floor to ceiling glass,
high above rush hour's blinking river.
We parted our lips for ambition's kiss
and woke with this glistening high-rise blister.

Ozymandian Towers – red on white.
Its façade has the cold-eyed glamour
of a lipsticked corpse on a quiet street.
At the reception desk, the empty chair.

A future, shiny as magazine paper,
dulled now to a finish blank and bare
as these windows; we glance inside, quick,
then laugh a laugh that's wet with despair.
Nothing to see
                    but ourselves staring back.

Plans

During his incarceration, Albert Speer
re-landscaped the garden of Spandau Prison.

I start with plans. Pencilled notes.
Dimensions of walkways, widths of beds.
I see pink azalea,
slender blue iris, white rose.
Names of flowers like the names
of beautiful women warm my lips.
Ripe plums. Red-gold apples.
Stones shaped by storms.
And I author, angel, god.

A man who sees things
as they could be.
Is this the man
I chose to be?

The other prisoners laugh at me.
Number Five, the yapping pup.
Give him the run of the garden,
keep him out of our hair.
I like to keep busy,
smell the damp earth.

In my dreams a girl
in white, with shining hair,
laughs. Does not call me *Number Five*
but *Albert.*
Hands me Berlin
in the shape of an apple.
I close my fingers
on its warm weight. Wake.

Yes. I'm the man
I chose to be.
A man who saw,
not what was,
but only what could be.

I started with plans.

Storm in Athens

December, 2008

Lightning makes the coldest light;
shows me the laurel tree as it flails
against the window, black
fruit like eyes peering in.
Shows me us in bed
not touching, clutching
the blanket's satin edge.

This storm is sex sounds
behind the wall, a biker
battering a car roof with his helmet,
feral cats showing claws
yards from the floodlit Acropolis.
It's light-up Santas outside shops
full of prayer beads and life-size wooden cocks.
It's the skeleton of the Christmas tree
the rioters set fire to,
a cab driver shouting *Call the Mister!*
Broken glass and water rising.
REO Speedwagon's Greatest Hits.

The lightning shows me myself –
over-ripe, easily bruised.

What can we mean by *justice*
when history's heavy fruit
bends our branches to the ground?
How can I hear you
above my heart's own feral sounds?

The Past

I.

The reindeer waits by the frozen lake
for the Lapp herders' signal. White wreaths
of breath form in the air and break.

The reindeer waits; the only sound
the snort and stir of the herd
he leads. The long ribbon of brown.

The herders wave and shout,
coax the leader onto the ice.
At first he keeps his head up, shows no doubt.

Then, with the shore in sight, the deer just
stops. Widens his eyes, sniffs the air.
The whole herd pauses on the lake's cold crust.

The reindeer turns, back toward where
he came from. What does he see?
Something draws him back there.

The herd tries to follow, turns back around,
but takes too long. The ice cracks.
The water's too cold. All the reindeer drown.

II.

Rob's therapist tells him:
The villains from our childhoods are wraiths
that haunt us, till we face them down.
Just have faith.

On the phone I've heard
how the ghosts are wearing Rob out.
He sounds tired, his voice blurred.

I worry about the price
of reopening the past;
that pain can mesmerize.

Rob's resurrecting memories
and I'm glad, if it's ground
he can stand on. And be free.

The past is a frozen lake.
If we linger, the ice will break.

The Way You Die Again In My Dreams

for Chuck

You slide away from me
down into the orange
winter evening.

The runners of your sled
sing, "Shush…shush."

I stay behind on the hilltop,
as still as the black barked trees.

My fingers are stiff with cold.
I never see you reach the bottom.

As still as the black barked trees,
I stay behind on the hilltop.

"Shush…shush," sing
the runners of your sled.

Winter evening.
Down into the orange
you slide, away from me.

Outside The Crane Bar

for Ger Ward

I

Living depends on not knowing –
moonless blue, no stars to follow.
Between the cobbles, weeds are growing.
Living depends on not knowing
how suddenly life can go.
On seldom swimming past the shallows.
Living depends on not knowing.
Moonless blue, no stars to follow.

II

Streetlamps make the scene look frail.
In the square, stilled by chains and rust,
the old cattle market scale.
Streetlamps make the scene frail –
solid iron looks spectral, pale.
Gone the hands that worked it, as hands must.
Streetlamps make it sepia, frail.
The scale is stilled by chains and rust.

III

Long gone are the hands
that hoisted hooves, bellies, heads –
creatures missing open land.
Long gone the many hands,
the cows' complaints. The scale now stands
near honking cars instead.
Who thinks of the many hands
that measured hooves, bellies, heads?

IV

Living depends on not knowing
so in the Crane they're busy forgetting.
Hands on pints. Fairy lights glowing.
Living depends on not knowing
that even as they're here they're going,
dying each minute – it's too upsetting.
Take refuge in not knowing.
In the Crane they're busy forgetting.

V

You should go too – back inside
where poets almost rhyme and fiddlers play,
where laughter forces grief to hide.
Come on, let's go back inside.
Tomorrow, the dead will still be dead,
and we'll fold our hands and we'll try to pray.
For now, please, let's go back inside
where poets almost rhyme and fiddlers play.

Penitents

The houses on Prospect Hill
kneel like penitents.
An old woman, picked clean,
whispers in the washroom
of Ceannt Station.

The man at the bus stop asks if
I am lonely.
His red t-shirt strains against
his saggy belly.
We are far from home, he says.
I'm Pakistani.
You're from the US, yes? From this
he thinks he knows me.
But I am picked clean.

We're on the lip of the Square, face
into its mouth.
Its beery breath, its twilight sighs.
The Angelus.
My family has disowned me,
the Pakistani says.

The houses on Prospect Hill
kneel like penitents,
picked clean.

Going At It

Saturday's trinity:
clothesline, lawnmower, sink.
A new ache in my back.
Mr. H. blows me a kiss.
I feel it land, flutter
like a moth against my neck.

Our neighbour's mouth is stuck
in a permanent "O".
"Mrs. H! Did you see them?
Three o'clock this morning!
Young couple on the green,
going at it!"

She happened to look
out her bedroom window.
Her face is flushed, her hands fisted.
"The wretch's arms thrown open
like Jesus on the cross.
Shameless!
I should've phoned the Guards."

I bite my lip, remember
our first summer;
the night I lifted my dress
in Father Burke Park –
the scrabbly grass, his sudden
cool flesh. Who watched,
I wonder, from which dark window…
how long ago?

How long have I been this housewife
who hangs laundry as it grows dark?
And when was the last time I asked Mr. H.
to take a walk in the park?

Ten Years In

and intimacy turns out not to be
the amber-lit bubble bath you pictured
in your sad-girl-bed-sit days –
but a hundred watt bulb. Bared.

You see now that the best of him
and worst of him
meet in the middle, like
two ends of one scarf.

He wore a scarf first time you met him.
An orange Dr. Who number.
He was scrawny and sad looking,
grateful for a dry place to sleep.

And you'll never stop trying
to save him from himself.
This morning you've sent him to the doctor
to get the tests a man his age gets.

You've become, God help you,
a middle-aged-married-lady.
Bye-bye bubble bath;
hello to the pleasures of love
in unflattering light.

Granny

Here's the thing – *rescued*.
Who said I needed rescue?
I can slice my own way
out of a wolf's belly.
Keep a nail file in my pocket –
learned that as a girl.
I'm not afraid of blood,
darkness or hard work.
I know the sticky sucking sound,
the rush of air and light,
the slide through the smiling wound
back into life.

Cries the Woodsman, *you're rescued!*
Who said I needed rescue?
I decide when it's time
to leave the sheltering cell behind,
return to the surface.

Sings my grandchild, *we're rescued!*
She still believes in rescues.
Slips her red cape onto his shoulders –
now he's Superman, grins
as he holds her.
That's her life decided.

The cottage is quiet
after they go –
dead dog in the bed,
sawdust on the lino...

I don't need a hero
for the rescue, but after;
to hold the dustpan, kiss my hair,
call me his Angel.

Missing Tom

If you stay awake you can have him back.
Wait here on the lamplit shore of night.
Beyond the reach of light wings spread,
paws find purchase, yellow eyes track.
Scrabble-tap. Small lives in dry grass.

Wait here.
If you step outside your hands will stretch
and sway like fern and frond,
helpless in the drag of tide; your mouth imitate
the circle of moon, your voice become
the night bird's cry.

If you stay awake he will come back,
slinking in, like sunrise through the letter box.
But if you sleep he will stay on, enthralled
by the musk of the wild; he is, after all,
its child.

Taillights

Shopping finished, I tend
to the trolley.

Mommy! No childish
whine — a howl.
Lift my hand to shield my eyes.
Scan the car park like a lifeguard.

There she is. No more
than nine. Chasing
a car. Chasing a car?
Banging on the boot
with small fists.
It glides just ahead
of her. The dusty blue sedan.

A cluster of us gather
on the concrete shore.
One woman points.
"Oh my God," says another.
The car nears the exit,
child still behind, tethered
by a lead invisible.

Mommy! Mommy wait! I see
hands taming the child's cloud
of curls this morning, catching
them in a pink band. These hands
now on the steering wheel.

It's a kind of suicide
to drive away — feel the seal
close behind you on your
Tupperwared life. Start again.

I wish I didn't
understand so well
how this might feel.

Because in my dreams, I am that
girl. Running.
My eyes full of taillights.
And the back of a head.

Connie

for Connie Culp of Hopedale, Ohio;
first US recipient of a face transplant

He steals her face, takes her teeth clean and white,
bone-sure and even as the town she lives in.
He turns the gun on himself after that.

Takes one brown eye, a nose that is straight.
Everything between eyelid and chin.
He steals her face, takes her teeth clean and white.

Who is she then? Who would you be, without
the verse of your features, the page of your skin?
He turns the gun on himself after that.

It's dark. Can't taste, can't talk, no breath.
Pain blooms stubborn as dandelions.
He steals her face, takes her teeth clean and white.

Renovation work must be done bit by bit.
(Connie has thirty operations.)
He turned the gun on himself after that.

New skin seals in all that came before.
What hurts us doesn't leave us; shapes us, beneath.
He stole her face, took her teeth clean and white;
turned the gun on himself after that.

Beatrice

Petals curl up, blow away
across the garden, like pale wings.
Poets steal faces, take voices away.

Dead-eyed masks underfoot decay –
beautiful, fleshless, silent things.
Petals curl up, blow away.

Excavate Beatrice; hold her so sky
pours through her lips. Pretend that she sings.
Poets steal faces, take voices away.

Imagine she sings of what filled her days.
Released from his rhyme, she tells everything.
Petals curl up, blow away.

And now the breeze is built of sighs
as mute women shake off sleep that clings.
Poets steal faces, take voices away.

Richer than what a poet will say
is what a woman can say of herself.
Petals curl up, blow away.
Poets steal faces, take voices away.

I Dream of Stephen Fry

He kisses me – I know,
I know. But it's my dream and
he kisses me. First he gazes down
at me – he is very, very tall –
with his painfully wise
sympathetic eyes. Tells me
we must face what is happening
between us. His voice is an oboe
with an English accent. Then
he kisses me. It goes on
and on. His mouth the perfect
moistness, his saliva Champagne.
Did I mention he wears a tux?
He presses me up against
a classic Roman column –
probably holding
up a building, I didn't
notice. The stone's been warmed
by a setting sun that gilds
the scene, as Fitzgerald
would say, like a benediction.
Somewhere church bells ring.

Don't analyse. No, Stephen Fry
does not resemble my father.
No I don't seek validation
by turning a homosexual.
Let's not talk about little girl
dreams of horses, or boy bands,
safe fantasy objects. That's not
what this is. What it is, is

somewhere there should be a place
where men with clean fingernails
who can name King Lear's daughters
look good in a tux
and have sympathetic eyes
wait to, want to, need to
kiss someone like me. As the sun sets,
like a benediction,
and somewhere, church bells ring.

I Dream My Mouth

is a crusted wound.
A galaxy in my throat.
Stars spill past my lips,
sharp enough to draw my blood
but how they sparkle. Oh, look!

Rooms

Rooms in dreams are usually women…
Sigmund Freud

The sky drips milk. People catch it in cups,
in bowls, on tongues. Fearing they're forsaken,
cows lower their great heads and sob.

Like the cows I'm heavy, aching
with something unexpressed. The white rain
falls cold. I shiver and quake,

slip in through an open door. Not mine.
Another's house. I wander room to room.
The forlorn mooing starts to wane

or rather is transformed, from boom
to whimper, distant to close by −
muffled cries, inside this stranger's home.

I think if it had been a boy
I would've named him Leaf. But then,
in this Fall, he would just have blown away.

Crusts of toast, empty mugs in the kitchen.
Ordinary. Coats hung in the hall.
Green carpet on the stairs. Those sobs again,

closer. I don't know should I call
out, offer help, a shoulder. I'm not
supposed to be here, after all,

and what will happen if I'm caught?
But I have to look behind each door,
can't stop. Something here that I forgot.

I think if it had been a girl
I would've named her Summer. But then,
she wouldn't be here anymore.

I pause at a window to watch the rain –
at my feet the first bright drops bloom,
mark the pale rug with deep red stains.

I don't wake up. Life does not resume.
Someone still sobs. I still walk room to room.

Breakfast

Coffee

Was thin and bitter;
brown dust and boiled water.

Her spoon clanked as she questioned
why the world had turned against her.

Life in its overcoat shuffled past
our windows' yellowed blinds.
That summer the breeze smelled of tar.
The mug smooth as bone
in her dishworn hands.

The coffee I pour into my own cup
tingles like neck kisses now,
lifts me up.

Italian, expensive; every sip moves me
from the overlooked people we were.
But I know, as I linger in this greener breeze
it takes me further away from her.

Juliet's Roommate Speaks

She's in the kitchen,
fingering her knives.
Her latest Romeo has drunk
from the poison cup,
so she's rummaging through cutlery.
Barefoot, hair tumbled.
Her frantic breath fogs the blades.
Oh happy dagger! she cries.

How I wish she'd date
a Mike or Joe;
tell the Romeos
where to go.

WAY OUT

I still see her sometimes – that pudgy
Philly girl in black eyeliner
and the Union Jack t-shirt
who had never been anywhere
worth being.

She takes pictures
of all the doors in Heathrow
because instead of EXIT
they are labelled WAY OUT.
This to her is hippie-
jazz speak.
Groovy, far out, *way out*, man!
Finally, a sign
of a cooler, warmer world.

London disappoints her – another
dirty city. She buys postcards,
gets her butt pinched on the Tube.
But WAY OUT
glows against the dark.

She's only seventeen and she's hardly
been anywhere except in her mind.
I still glimpse her sometimes
in storefront windows. She knows nothing
and too much. All I want to do
is hug her and promise
it does get better.
You will find a way out.
Someday.

St. Louis, November 2008

He stood right there
on that bald patch of grass.
I was working,
got real close.

Behind us, the Mississippi
slaps the bank. Before us, the hard dome
of St. Louis Courthouse.
Slaves were auctioned
on its side door steps.

Dred Scott sued for his freedom here –
the Supreme Court called him "an ordinary
article of merchandise".

It's been raining –
the field looks battered.
But feel how soft the soil is,
how it yields.

I got real close,
had a great view.
The black security guard
smiles as he remembers.
More than
a hundred thousand people.
History? *Well,*
I think so.

I Learn To Write

S is a rolling ocean,
U a moonless valley.
Seduced by its geography
And dizzy with pride I print my name
Neatly down the page.

Declare myself a continent.
Undo their colonization.
Make my flag
And fly it.
Really me now.
Separate.

Skates

Morning is a blank wall, hot and white,
hurts your eyes, you want to write
all over it. You can wreck stuff
just by looking at it. *Get away*
Mom says, *out of my sight*.

Skinny clouds, cracks in the sky.
Mom laces up your skates – ties
a thousand knots. *Now. Go!*
No one around. Maybe
everyone has died.

Maybe if you yell
you can CRASH
                    break
                            the blue shell.
Mom will hit you
if you bust the sky.
Your teeth hurt from the *ka-ka-ka*,
pebbles in your wheels.

Your feet are hot
but the knots won't come out.
The sky is a shell.
Your skin is a shell.
Break it.

There must be something inside
that everyone would love to touch

and say *Aahh*
some small good thing

and it would fly above the pavement
over the houses and Mom would yell
but the good thing would laugh and all
the people, they would wave.

But no Man moved Me — till the Tide

Crawl inside this line —
hear the heartbeat rush of waves.

Cold, proud.
                Cold, proud.

Brides of the sea — me and
Emily. In our white
dresses turning towards, not away
from love. Fresh and fast as ocean spray,
the words —
silver heel, solid town,
dandelion, pearl.
Turning towards
the lines, the beat, the tide.

We dive into
the language sea.

(Inspired by #520, by Emily Dickinson)

Plato's Ghost

All his happier dreams came true –
A small old house, wife, daughter, son,
Grounds where plum and cabbage grew,
Poets and Wits about him drew;
"What then?" sang Plato's ghost, "what then?"

William Butler Yeats

He often croons in my ear too
his impossible vision;
not about fields where cabbage grew
but why I can't make cabbage stew –
"What's for dinner?" sings Plato's ghost.

Just when I think I can relax
comes the sneering apparition
and points out ways I have been lax –
empty fridge, nothing for snacks.
"But what's for dinner?" sings Plato's ghost.

Not only for those I have not fed
am I burned by his derision;
but for the kids I never had,
the I love yous I never said.
"Aren't you hungry?" sings Plato's ghost.

I'm selfish more than I am sweet;
have nourished my own wisdom.
Poets and Wits I often meet
but don't give them a thing to eat.
And louder sang that ghost, "What's for dinner?"

Make Me an Instrument

Why can't I be the old man so still on the green
in a circle of flung breadcrumbs,
waiting for the seagulls?
See them lined up on my neighbour's roof,
a row of semi-colons; watch them lift off,
soar, bellies yellowed by the low sun –
have them come to me?

Why can't I be St. Francis,
birds brushing the hem of my tunic?
The wolf's trusting paw in my hand?
Why can't I meet the world halfway,
be free of everything but faith,
feel the low sun,
like love, warm on my skin?

If I could be the old man
who smiles
and waits,

would words lift off,
soar,
flock to me?

Ladybug

Lands
on my arm
in the warm crease
of elbow.
Red.
Tender, snug.

Takes me from
hard-edged thoughts,
reminds me
sometimes strength
is soft.

Sun on my face.
Little
by little
I learn
to melt.

#30 Mexico Plum

for Kevin

The flame touch
soft wet tickle
of brush-stroke
on toes –
he gives me
coat after coat,
lavender becoming
purple, becoming
blood-black.

I wriggle, white
above ten
tiny canvasses.

And all winter
beneath my solemn socks
and waterproof boots
I'll know my toes
wear *#30 Mexico Plum*
party hats. That's
what he gives me.

Philadelphia, August 1966

I was lucky; wombed
in the woman with the cat's eye
glasses, the chic French twist

at the Beatles' concert. Their last tour. A hot day.
The band miles away across a field
pristine as astronauts' dreams of the moon.

Can't buy me love
just a rumble-squeak beneath
the horny joyful screams.
The young one behind my mother sobs *Paul,*
Paul.

Mom doesn't scream. Her husband
beside her, pens in his breast pocket. His hair
just beginning to lick at his ears.

He owns a guitar, my dad; it leans
against the living room wall, like a moon
he plans to visit.

Her moon, me. First roundness, first flag
on Planet Family. She steals looks
at my handsome father
and loves him. *Yeah yeah yeah.*

She believes in him and
he believes in him and
the moon is waiting.
Anything is possible.

I was made from this.

Blessing

Evening. Light loosens its grip.
Saints gather, clouds in their hair –
wish for flesh enough to feel
this warm June rain. Soft air.
Walking, through wet streets,
home. Here I am. Here
I want to be.

About the Author

Susan Millar DuMars was born in Philadelphia in 1966. Her debut poetry collection, *Big Pink Umbrella*, was published by Salmon Poetry in 2008. *Dreams for Breakfast* is her second collection. Her work appears in *The Best of Irish Poetry 2010* and *Landing Places: Immigrant Poets in Ireland* (2010). A fiction writer as well, she  published a collection of short stories, *American Girls*, with Lapwing in 2007, and is at work on a further story collection. Susan has been the recipient of an Arts Council Literature Bursary. She lives in Galway, where she works as a creative writing teacher. Susan and her husband, Kevin Higgins, have run Galway's Over the Edge readings series since its inception in 2003.